CONTENTS

INTRODUCTION TO A CHRISTMAS CAROL

COMMON THEMES

Dickens wrote **15** novels and many shorter works with themes such as;

- SOCIETY & CLASS
- POVERTY, INJUSTICE & CRIME
- FAMILY
- LIFE, DEATH & REDEMPTION
- WEALTH, GREED &
- BENEVOLENCE (GENEROSITY)
- RELIGION & CHRISTMAS

REAL WORLD

- Scrooge's office
- Scrooge's house
- The Cratchit's house
- Fred's house

WHEN?

'A Christmas Carol' is a novella (short novel) published in 1843, consisting of 5 chapters or **STAVES**. He wrote it in response to the appalling living conditions he had witnessed in the slums.

WHO WROTE IT?

Charles Dickens - Author.

Born in 1812 in Kent, one of eight children.

His father was sent to a debtor's prison in London & his family followed.

When the family moved to the same prison, Charles stayed with a family friend, where (aged 12), he was sent to work in a blacking (shoe polish) factory.

He was able to return to education when his Great Grandmother left the family money.

After his education, he worked as a low clerk, married & had ten children.

SETTING

Victorian London - a place of inequality, poverty & filth.

LOCATIONS

VISIONS

- Scrooge's school in the countryside
- Fezziwig's office/party
- Mine/lighthouse

CHARACTER OVERVIEW. WHO'S WHO & WHAT THEY DO

THE THREE SPIRITS

GHOST OF CHRISTMAS PAST

Magical in appearance, childlike & old, it shows Scrooge scenes from his past & reawakens old memories.

GHOST OF CHRISTMAS PRESENT

A giant, jolly & festive figure who shows Scrooge the joy that others find in celebrating Christmas.

GHOST OF CHRISTMAS YET TO COME

A grim, unspeaking & mysterious spirit, shrouded in 'deep black'. It shows Scrooge what will happen to him & others if he doesn't change his ways.

IGNORANCE & WANT

PRESENT - Two starving children cowering under Ghost of Christmas Present's gown.

FUTURE - The Corpse/Businessmen/ Young Couple & Mrs Dilber.

JACOB MARLEY'S SPIRIT - The spirit of Scrooge's dead business partner. Like Scrooge he spent his life alone & valued wealth above all. He warns Scrooge he will be haunted by 3 ghosts.

EBENEZER SCROOGE

(Main character) A wealthy, miserly & bitter old man. Protagonist

BOB CRATCHIT, TINY TIM & FAMILY

BOB- Scrooge's hard working clerk. Warm, uncomplaining & young at heart.

TINY TIM- Bob's physically impaired son, happy & loving.

FRED - Scrooge's nephew. He loves Christmas & is generous, never giving up on Scrooge.

BELLE- Scrooge's sweetheart from his youth. They were engaged to be married, but she couldn't compete with is first love - money!

CHARACTERS FROM VISIONS

PAST

YOUNG SCROOGE- lonely at school/in love with Belle.

FAN- Scrooge's sister - she brings young Scrooge home from school for Christmas.

FEZZIWIG- Scrooge's old boss, generous, a love of Christmas.

2

PLOT & STRUCTURE. THE STORY IN FIVE STAVES

1 - MARLEY'S GHOST

Scrooge & his clerk Bob Cratchit are working on Christmas Eve. Scrooge's nephew (Fred) invites Scrooge for Christmas dinner, but he refuses & sends a man collecting for charity away.

At home, Marley's Ghost appears (first on a door knocker, later in Scrooge's room) & gives Scrooge a warning; unless he changes his ways, he is destined to roam the earth endlessly. Three ghosts will visit to help him save himself.

2 - THE FIRST OF THE THREE SPIRITS

The Ghost of Christmas Past appears & shows Scrooge visions of his past; Christmas as a lonely boy at school & sister fan taking him home, Christmas as a young apprentice celebrating at his boss Fezziwig's party, his fiancé Belle breaking off their engagement & Belle years on with a family of her own. Scrooge is upset & begs the ghost to stop, finally waking in his bed.

3 - THE SECOND OF THE THREE SPIRITS

The Ghost of Christmas Present appears & shows Scrooge how others are spending Christmas. eg. the Cratchits enjoying their simple Christmas together. They visit Fred's house where the guests make fun of Scrooge & he discovers Tiny Tim will die in the future. Two starving children 'Want & Ignorance' cower beneath the ghost's robes & Scrooge is warned of the dangers of ignoring them.

4 - THE LAST OF THE THREE SPIRITS

The Ghost of Christmas Yet to Come appears to Scrooge & shows people discussing a man who has died & thieves stealing his stuff. Scrooge is too frightened to reveal the corpse's face. Next they travel to the Cratchit's home, where they are mourning Tiny Tim's death. Finally the ghost shows Scrooge a grave-stone with his name on it. He promises he will change his ways.

5 - THE END OF IT

Scrooge wakes in bed, happy to discover it is still Christmas day. He is excited to change & shouts Christmas greetings to those he meets. He orders a turkey to be sent to the Cratchit's home & he gives money to charity. He joins his nephew for Christmas dinner & the next day gives Bob a pay rise. We are told that Scrooge changed his ways for good & as a result, Tiny Tim lives a long life.

EBENEZER SCROOGE

THE NARRATOR DESCRIBES HIM AS...

MISERLY -
'Scrooge! a squeezing, wrench -ing, grasping, scraping, clutching covetous old sinner!'

TOUGH -
'Hard and sharp as flint, from which no steel had ever struck out a generous fire.'

ALONE -
'... secret, and self-contained, and solitary as an oyster.'

COLD-HEARTED -
'He carried his own low temper -ature always about with him; he iced his office.'

'No warmth could warm, no wintry weather chill him.'

HARD EDGED -
'The cold within him froze his old features, nipped his pointed nose, shrivelled his cheek, stiffened his gait; made his eyes red, his thin lips blue.'

DREADED -
'Scrooge was the Ogre of the family. The mention of his name cast a dark shadow on the party....'

WHAT OTHERS SAY ABOUT HIM ....

"Odious, stingy, hard unfeeling man." (Mrs Cratchit)

"Merciless creditor" (The couple in debt to him)

"Old scratch" - name for the devil (A businessman)

"He has given us plenty of merriment I am sure." (As a subject of ridicule - Fred)

WHO IS HE?

'Oh! But he was a tight fisted hand at the grindstone.'

- A wealthy & miserly businessman.
- Alone, unmoved & unloved.
- Blames the poor for their poverty.

HIS OWN WORDS -

UNSYMPATHETIC TO POOR -
"If they would rather die," said Scrooge, "they had better do it and decrease the surplus population."

LACKS CHRISTMAS SPIRIT -
"Every idiot that goes about with 'Merry Christmas' on his lips should be boiled with his own pudding."

RESENTFUL -
"A poor excuse for picking a man's pocket every twenty-fifth of December."

UNCHARITABLE -
"I can't afford to make idle people merry."

UNBELIEVING -
"You may be an undigested bit of beef." (to Ghost of Marley)

EMOTIONALLY DISTANT -
the clerk. (his long standing employee Bob)

REJECTS FAMILY -
"Bah!" said Scrooge. "Humbug!" (rejecting Fred's invitation to Christmas dinner)

RESPECTS MARLEY -
"Yes! Yes! You were always a good friend to me, Jacob! MARLEY."

4

The story shows us his transformation as he becomes...

A REDEEMED MAN –

"I hope to live to be another man from what I was."

EMPATHETIC – "Have they no refuge or resource?" cried Scrooge. (At 'Ignorance & Want').

DETERMINED TO MAKE A DIFFERENCE – 'He was so fluttered and so glowing with his good intentions.'

JOYFUL – "I am light as a feather, I am as happy as an angel." (Scrooge)

GENEROUS & HUMOROUS – "I am not going to stand this... And therefore... I am about to raise your salary.' (Scrooge to Bob).

A MAN OF HIS WORD – 'Scrooge was better than his word. He did it all, and infinitely more.' (Narrator)

The visions he is shown by the three Spirits/Ghosts reawaken emotion & he is....

SAD – 'Scrooge said he knew it. And he sobbed.'(At seeing himself as a boy).

How SCROOGE CHANGES

REGRETFUL – 'Scrooge seemed uneasy in his mind.'(At the thought of his nephew). (Narrator).

IN PAIN – "show me no more!... why do you delight to torture me?" (Scrooge)

PENITENT – 'Scrooge was... overcome with penitence and grief.' (Tim's death). (Narrator)

Scrooge's trip to the past shows us he wasn't always miserly & cold hearted.

As a boy he was.....

LONELY – 'A solitary child, neglected by his friends.' (Ghost of Christmas Past)

IMAGINATIVE – "Why it's Ali Baba!" Scrooge exclaimed in ecstasy.

LOVED – "I have come to bring you home, dear brother!" said the child. (Fan)

NEGLECTED – "Father is so much kinder than he used to be."

As a young man, he was.....

LOVED – "He was very much attached to me, was Dick...." "...a fair young girl in a mourning dress: in whose eye there were tears." (Narrator)

HE CARED – "Why it's old Fezziwig! Bless his heart." (Scrooge)

CHANGED – "Another idol has displaced me ....A golden one." (Belle)

BOB CRATCHIT

ABUSED
'...his clerk's fire was so very much smaller ...But he couldn't replenish it.' (Narrator)

UNCOMPLAINING
'...the clerk put on his white comforter, and tried to warm himself at the candle.' (Narrator)

PROUD
'...his threadbare clothes darned up & brushed, to look seasonable.'

OPTIMISTIC
'...my clerk, with fifteen shillings a week, and a wife and family, talking about a merry Christmas.' (Scrooge)

A FAMILY MAN
'...the two young Cratchit's go upon his knees and laid, each child a little cheek against his face.' (Narrator)

LOVING & PROTECTIVE
'Bob held his withered little hand in his, as if he loved the child ...and dreaded that he might be taken from him.' (Narrator)

WHO IS HE?
'...his clerk, who in a dismal little cell beyond a sort of tank, was copying letters.' (Narrator)

- Scrooge's poorly treated clerk.
- Uncomplaining & optimistic.
- A loving & hardworking father & husband.

CHARACTER CHANGE?
Bob's character remains constant but his life is impacted through Scrooge's transformation. eg- Bob's pay rise (& Scrooge's intervention in Tiny Tim's life as a second father).

YOUNG AT HEART
'The clerk ...went down a slide at Cornhill... twenty times.' (Narrator)

DIGNIFIED
'...we shall not quarrel easily among ourselves and forget poor Tiny Tim in doing it.' (Bob)

GRIEF-STRICKEN
'My little, little child!' cried Bob 'My little child!'

6

JACOB MARLEY

IN DEATH

FRIGHTENING -
'the chilling influence', 'death cold eyes', 'lower jaw dropped down upon its breast.' (Narrator)

WEARS BURDEN OF MONEY -
'...long and wound about him like a tail; and it was made ...of cash- boxes, keys, padlocks, ledgers, deeds and heavy purses wrought in steel.'

TORTURED -
"I cannot rest, I cannot stay, I cannot linger anywhere."

GUILT-RIDDEN -
"no rest, no peace. Incessant torture of remorse."

SELF AWARE -
"I wear the chain I forged in life... I made it link by link... and of my own free will I wore it."

REGRETFUL -
"Mankind should have been my business."

CHANGED -
"No space of regret can make amends for one life's opportunity misused."

REDEEMED -
"You have yet a chance and a hope of escaping my fate."

DESPERATE -
"Hear me! my time is nearly gone."

IN LIFE

ALONE -
'Scrooge was his sole executor ...his sole friend, and sole mourner.' (Narrator)

UNLOVED -
'And even Scrooge was not so dreadfully cut up by the sad event...' (Narrator)

OBSESSED -
"My spirit never walked beyond our counting house."

WHO IS HE ?

- 'Marley was dead: to begin with.'

- The ghost of Scrooge's business partner who warns Scrooge against turning out like him.

- He appears first as a door knocker then in heavy chains in Scrooge's room.

- He warns that Scrooge 'will be haunted' by three ghosts, his chain more ponderous than Marley's.

CHARACTER CHANGE?

When we meet Marley, he has already seen the error of his ways (placing more value on wealth than people). He hopes Scrooge will change while he still has time to make a difference.

GHOST OF CHRISTMAS PAST

BEAUTIFUL
'It wore a tunic of the purest white; and round its waist was bound a lustrous belt, the sheen of which was beautiful.' (Narrator)

TIMELESS
'...in singular contradiction of that wintry emblem, had its dress trimmed with summer flowers.' (Narrator)

REVEALING
'The curtains of his bed were drawn aside.' (Narrator)

ILLUMINATING
'...from the crown of its head there sprung a bright clear jet of light, by which all this was visible.' (Narrator)

CANDLELIKE
'a great extinguisher for a cap, ...which it now held under its arm.' (Narrator)

CHANGEABLE / CONTRADICTORY
'... what was light one instant, at another time was dark, so the figure itself fluctuated in its distinctness.' (Narrator)

SUPERNATURAL
'Scrooge ... found himself face to face with the unearthly visitor.' (Narrator)

AGELESS
'It's hair... was white as if with age; and yet the face had not a wrinkle on it.' (Narrator)

WHO?
'It was a strange figure - like a child: yet not so like a child as like an old man.'

- An ageless & contradictory figure who takes Scrooge to revisit his past & reawakens old emotions.

FORCEFUL
'But the relentless Ghost pinioned him in both arms, and forced him to observe.' (Narrator)

BENEVOLENT
'He then made bold to inquire what business brought him there.' "Your welfare" said the Ghost.' (Narrator)

PROBING
'"What's the matter?' Something I think?"' (Ghost of Christmas Past)

SCROOGE'S REACTION

MEMORY -
'... a thousand thoughts, and hopes, and joys and cares long, long, forgotten!'

FORGOTTEN JOY -
'Bless his heart, it's Fezziwig alive again!'

PAIN/SADNESS -
'"Spirit" said Scrooge in a broken voice, "remove me from this place."'

REGRET -
'"I wish," Scrooge muttered ... but it's too late now."'

AVOIDANCE -
'"Show me no more! Conduct me home. Why do you delight to torture me?"' (Tries to snuff spirit out)

8

GHOST OF CHRISTMAS PRESENT

FRIENDLY
"Come in! and know me better, man!"

GENEROUS
'he shed a few drops of water... and their good humour was restored.' (Narrator)

HOPEFUL
'... many homes they visited but always with a happy end.' (Narrator)

HONEST
'... its capacious breast was bare, as if disdaining to be... concealed by any artifice.' (Narrator)

FORBODING
"I see a vacant seat... the child will die."
"They are man's... Beware them both."

SORROWFUL
"It might be a claw, for the flesh there is upon it." was the spirit's sorrowful reply.

STERN
"slander those who tell it ye!"

AGEING
'...the Ghost grew older...'My life upon this globe, is very brief... it ends to-night." (Narrator)

COMMANDING
'... a strange voice called him by his name and bade him enter. He obeyed.' (Narrator)

ABUNDANT
'Heaped up on the floor, to form a kind of throne, were turkeys, geese and game.'

WHO?
'There sat a jolly Giant, glorious to see; who bore a glowing torch... to shed its light on Scrooge.' (Narrator)

- A warm and joyous figure who shows Scrooge different Christmases in different places.

SCROOGE'S REACTION

WILLING -
"conduct me where you will." (Scrooge)
"... if you have aught to teach me, let me profit by it." (Scrooge)

SHAME -
'Scrooge hung his head to hear his own words quoted by the Spirit, and was overcome with penitence and grief.' (Narrator)

QUESTIONING -
"You would deprive them of their means of dining every seventh day... wouldn't you?" (Scrooge)

DEFERENCE -
"Forgive me I am wrong. It had been done in your name..." (Scrooge)

APPRECIATES CHRISTMAS -
"Here is a new game" said Scrooge. "One half hour, Spirit, only one!"

EMPATHY -
"Spirit," said Scrooge, with an interest he had never felt before, "tell me if Tiny Tim will live."

9

GHOST OF CHRISTMAS YET TO COME

FRIGHTENING
'Scrooge feared the silent shape so much that his legs trembled beneath him.' (Narrator)

OMINOUS
'...it seemed to scatter gloom and mystery.'
'The Unseen Eyes were looking at him keenly. It made him shudder.' (Narrator)

SYMBOL OF DEATH
'It was shrouded in a deep black garment which concealed its head ...and left nothing visible, save one out -stretched hand.' (Narrator)

GENTLE
'The Spirit paused a moment, as observing his condition, and giving him time to recover.'

FEELING
'The kind hand trembled.' (Narrator)

DIRECT
'The finger pointed from the grave to him, and back again.' (Narrator)

UNSPEAKING
'The Spirit neither spoke nor moved.' (Narrator)

UNHOLY
'Its mysterious presence filled him with a solemn dread.' (Narrator)

WHO?
'..a solemn Phantom, draped and hooded, coming like a mist along the ground, towards him.'

- An unspeaking and ominous spirit who shows Scrooge the future if he remains unchanged.

SCROOGE'S REACTION

FEAR- "I fear you more than any spectre I have seen."

SUBMISSIVENESS- 'When it came, Scrooge bent down upon his knee.'

OPEN- "I know your purpose is to do me good."
"I am prepared to bear you company, and do it with a thankful heart."

WISDOM- 'He thought if this man could be raised up now, what would be his foremost thoughts?'

CHANGED- "But if the course be departed from, the ends will change." (Ghost of Christmas Yet to Come)

UNRELENTING
"Spirit!" he said, "this is a fearful place. In leaving it, I shall not leave its lesson, trust me. Let us go." Still the Ghost pointed with an unmoved finger to the head.

'The inexorable finger underwent no change.'

RIP EBENEZER SCROOGE

10

FRED (SCROOGE'S NEPHEW)

LIKEABLE

"If you should happen ...to know a man ...more blest in a laugh than Scrooge's nephew... I should like to know him." (Narrator)

GODLY

"God save you!"

COMPASSIONATE

"I am sorry for him; I couldn't be angrier with him if I tried. Who suffers by his ill whims? Himself."

INSIGHTFUL

"his offences carry their own punishment."

FORGIVING

"I mean to give him the same chance, every year, whether he likes it or not."

HOSPITABLE

"Come! Dine with us tomorrow."

GENEROUS

'Bob told them of the extraordinary kindness of Mr Scrooge's nephew.' (Narrator)

LOVES CHRISTMAS

"a good time; a kind, forgiving, charitable, pleasant time" "A merry Christmas uncle!"

JOYFUL

"...he was all in a glow ...his eyes sparkled." (Narrator)

VALUES PEOPLE OVER MONEY

"I want nothing from you; I ask nothing of you; why cannot we be friends?"

DIRECT

"What reason do you have to be morose? You're rich enough."

WHO IS HE?

'... he was all in a glow; his face was ruddy and handsome; his eyes sparkled.' (Narrator)

- Scrooge's nephew (Fan's son) who never gives up on his uncle.

- He is Scrooge's 'foil' (total opposite). happy & compassionate.

- Persistently makes an effort with Scrooge, despite years of rejection.

CHARACTER CHANGE?

Fred is happy at Scrooge's transformation & makes him feel very welcome which is what his character would always have done.

PATIENT & PERSISTENT

"...he finds me going there, in good temper, year after year."

11

THE CRATCHIT FAMILY

VICTIM OF POVERTY
Malnutrition in Victorian Time caused disabilities such as rickets.

THOUGHTFUL / GODLY
"He told me... it might be pleasant to them to remember upon Christmas day who made lame beggars walk & blind men see." (Tiny Tim)

INSPIRING
'Spirit of Tiny Tim, thy childish essence was from God.' 'His active little crutch....' (Narrator)

MEMORABLE
'... we shall none of us forget poor Tiny Tim." (Bob)

GOOD NATURED
"...we recollect how patient and how mild he was." (Bob)

SOULFUL
'had a plaintive little voice, and sang it very well indeed.' (Narrator)

TINY TIM
The physically impaired son of Bob. His limbs supported by an iron frame.

KIND
"God bless us every one!" (Tiny Tim)

WHO ARE THEY?
- Loving, close, hardworking family.
- Though they are poor they are happy.
- They represent the love lacking in Scrooge's lonely existence, especially the father / son relationship.

'They were not a handsome family; they were not well dressed... But, they were happy, grateful, pleased with one another, and contented.' (Narrator)

MRS CRATCHIT

BRAVE
'hides her weak eyes' after Tim's death, 'steady, cheerful voice'. (Narrator)

RESOURCEFUL
'Cratchit's wife, dressed out but poorly in a twice-turned gown, but brave in ribbons, which are cheap and make a goodly show for sixpence.' (Narrator)

PROTECTIVE
"The Founder of the Feast indeed!" cried Mrs Cratchit, reddening. "I wish I had him here. I'd give him a piece of my mind to feast upon..."

THE OTHER CHILDREN
HARDWORKING - Martha
ASPIRATIONAL - Peter
JOYFUL & GRATEFUL - Belinda

RIP TINY TIM

12

ADDITIONAL CHARACTERS

THE POETRY (POOR?)

GENTLEMEN

CHARITABLE - "... a few of us are endeavouring to raise a fund to buy the poor some meat and drink..."

COMPASSIONATE - "... hundreds of thousands are in want of common comforts, sir."

HONOURABLE - "I will!" cried the old gentleman. And it was clear he meant to do it.

DICK WILKINS - Scrooge's friend

"Bless me, yes... He was very much attached to me was Dick."

IGNORANCE & WANT

SYMBOLS OF POVERTY - "From the foldings of its robe, it brought two children; wretched, abject, hideous, miserable." (narrator)

SHOCKING - "I see something strange and not belonging to yourself, protruding from your skirt. Is it a foot or claw?" (Scrooge)

THE BUSINESS MAN, YOUNG COUPLE & MRS DILBER show no sorrow at Scrooge's death.

MINOR CHARACTERS

FRED'S WIFE & PARTY GUESTS

DISLIKE SCROOGE - "I have no patience with him," observed Scrooge's niece. Scrooge's niece's sisters and all the other ladies expressed the same opinion.

FUN - "... they played at forfeits; for it is good to be children sometimes, and never better than at Christmas..."

FAN

Scrooge's sister & Fred's mother.

LOVING - "... addressed him as her "Dear, dear brother."

FORGIVING - "Father is so much kinder than he used to be..."

BRAVE - "... I was not afraid to ask him once more if you might come home..."

MR FEZZIWIG

ADMIRED - "Why, it's old Fezziwig! Bless his heart; it's Fezziwig alive again!" (Scrooge)

ENJOYED CHRISTMAS - "No more work to-night... Christmas, Ebenezer!" (Fezziwig)

JOYFUL - "Hilli-ho! cried Fezziwig, skipping down from the high desk, with wonderful agility... Chirrup, Ebenezer!"

BELLE

Scrooge's ex fiance

REJECTED - "Another idol has displaced me... a golden one."

INSIGHTFUL - "... would you seek me out and try to win me now?"

SELFLESS - "... I release you. With a full heart, for the love of him you once were."

OVERVIEW OF THEMES

They include...
- CHRISTMAS
- FAMILY & RELATIONSHIPS
- TIME
- REDEMPTION (LIFE & DEATH)
- SOCIAL INJUSTICE (POVERTY, WEALTH & GREED)

SOCIAL INJUSTICE

Scrooge (& Marley) love money above all else, but it doesn't bring happiness & can even lead to a life of misery. Love of money as the 'root of all evil' is a Christian ideology.

The poverty gap was increasing & with the industrialisation of cities in Britain, the rich enjoyed luxury, while the poor couldn't meet their basic needs of health, food & shelter. This was well before the welfare state, but Dickens explores the idea that those with money should support those without.

REDEMPTION

Marley begs Scrooge not to live a wasted life like him.

The Ghost of Christmas Yet to Come makes Scrooge face up to the reality of death - a grave stone, mourners & a corpse. Seeing how he has spent his life & how he will be remembered in death wakes Scrooge up to his own mortality & makes him question his life path. The visitations raise the question of whether a person can change.

TIME

A striking clock is used throughout to denote passing & finite time. Scrooge travels through time, visiting his past, present & future. Ideas of regret, wishing to change the past & the idea that the past shapes us are discussed.

CHRISTMAS

Through Scrooge & the Cratchits, Dickens evaluates the true meaning of Christmas & its value as the season of goodwill to all men.

It captures the change of Christmas becoming less religious & more secular & about trimmings associated with the perfect Christmas & spending time with family. It chronicles the gap between the 'have & have nots' & the sense that Christmas was a time for charitable good works.

FAMILY

The comparison of the loving Cratchit family & the lonely Scrooge shine a light on the joy family can bring, regardless of wealth. Scrooge's journey to the past reminds him of how close he become to being a father & husband. Towards the end of the novella Scrooge begins to realise all men are his brothers.

CHRISTMAS

A WASTE OF MONEY
"A poor excuse for picking a man's pocket every twenty-fifth of December." (Scrooge)

A CELEBRATION
"Yo ho, my boys!" said Fezziwig. "No more work to-night..." Christmas, Ebenezer!" (Narrator)

FUN
'There were more dances, and there were forfeits, and more dances, and there was cake.' (Narrator)

OPULENT
'Heaped up on the floor, to form a kind of throne, were turkeys... plum-puddings... immense twelfth-cakes...' (Narrator)

MAGNIFIES INEQUALITY
"we choose this time, because it is a time, of all others, when Want is keenly felt, and Abundance rejoices." (Portly Gentleman)

CHRISTMAS IS...

POINTLESS
"Bah!" said Scrooge "Humbug!"

FOOLISH
"Every idiot who goes about with 'Merry Christmas' on his lips should be boiled with his own pudding, and buried with a stake of holly through his heart." (Scrooge)

CONTEXT
- Victorian society was very religious; church attendance on the Sabbath & other religious days was key.
- A 'good Christian life' reflected 'good works', such as charity, kindness & forgiveness.
- Dickens is credited with the rise of Christmas celebrations as we know it.

DICKENS' VIEWPOINT
Dickens loved celebrating Christmas with his large family & wrote several Christmas themed stories, as well as his own musical carol.

Dickens had experienced both poverty & wealth in his life & knew that Christmas Day was the only day many families would eat well.

CHARITABLE
"At this festive season of the year, Mr. Scrooge," said the gentleman... "we should make some slight provision for the poor and destitute..." (Portly Gentleman)

ABOUT FAMILY
'Mrs. Cratchit entered - flushed, but smiling proudly - with the pudding.' (Narrator)

COMPASSIONATE
"a kind, forgiving, charitable, pleasant time,... when men and women seem by one consent to open their shut-up hearts freely." (Fred)

FOR EVERYONE
"It's Christmas Day!" said Scrooge.

SOCIAL INJUSTICE

THE POOR...

ARE A NUISANCE

"If they would rather die," said Scrooge "they had better do it and decrease the surplus population." (Scrooge)

HIDDEN

"Are there no prisons? ... Are there no workhouses?" (Scrooge)

ARE MANY

"...thousands are in want of common necessaries; hundreds of thousands are in want." (The Portly Gentleman)

LAZY

"I can't afford to make idle people merry." (Scrooge)

DIGNIFIED

"They were not a handsome family; they were not well dressed ... But, they were happy, grateful, pleased with one another, and contented." (Narrator)

ARE GREEDY

"...a squeezing, wrenching, grasping, scraping, clutching, covetous old sinner!" (Narrator)

ARE WASTEFUL

"...orders to his fifty cooks and butlers to keep Christmas as a lord Mayor's household should...." (Narrator)

THE WEALTHY...

ARE RESPONSIBLE

"Spirit! are they yours?" Scrooge could say no more. "They are Man's," said the Spirit. (Ghost of Christmas Present)

CAN HELP

"a few of us are endeavouring to raise a fund to buy the poor some meat and drink, and means of warmth..." (The Portly Gentleman)

CONTEXT

- During the Industrial Revolution people flocked to the cities, which led to slum living, disease & hunger amongst the poor. Education was only for the wealthy.

- Some sections of society believed that charity encouraged laziness & in 1834 a New Poor Law was passed so that food or shelter was only given to those entering workhouses.

- A Christmas Carol was conceived by Dickens as a story to draw attention to child poverty.

DICKENS' VIEWPOINT

When Dickens was 12 his father was imprisoned in a debtor's jail & Charles was forced to work in a 'blacking' factory to support his family.

This gave him an understanding of poverty & a belief that education was key in eradicating 'Ignorance & Want'. Dickens strongly opposed 'Sabbatarianism' because many poor families would only eat if the bakers baked bread.

16

REDEMPTION - LIFE & DEATH

CHANGES PEOPLE

"You are changed... when it was made, you were another man." (Belle)

SHOULD BE LIVED WELL

"...no space of regret can make amends for one's life's opportunity misused!" (Marley)

REFLECTS VALUES

"What idol has displaced you?" he rejoined. "A golden one." (Belle)

CAN BRING REGRET

"...when he thought that such another creature... might have called him father... his sight grew very dim indeed." (Narrator)

DEATH...

BRINGS JUDGEMENT

"It is required of every man," the Ghost returned, "that the spirit within him should walk abroad among his fellowmen..." (Marley)

LEADS TO AFTERLIFE

"I cannot rest, I cannot stay, I cannot linger anywhere..."
"...and if that spirit goes not forth in life, it is condemned to do so after death." (Marley)

CONTEXT

- For Victorians, death was a harsh reality, with the average lifespan being approximately 29 years.

- Christianity was the prominent faith of the time & many believed that the soul immortal & the existence of 'an afterlife'.

LIFE... IS A CHOICE

"I wear the chain I forged in life," replied the Ghost. "I made it link by link, and yard by yard; I girded it on of my own free will." (Marley)

DICKENS' VIEWPOINT

Dickens disliked 'fire and brimstone' religious teachings, but did express belief in the bible & wrote that heaven 'was where we hope to go.'

He felt a 'great responsibility' upon him for the welfare of human beings.

CHANGES

"Spirit!" he cried, clutching at its robe, "hear me! I am not the man I was." (Scrooge)

IS DIFFICULT

"No more!" cried Scrooge. "No more. I don't wish to see it. Show me no more!"

REDEMPTION... CAN BE SOUGHT

'He then made bold to inquire what business brought him there. "Your welfare!" said the Ghost ... "Your reclamation." (Ghost of Christmas Past)

TRANSFORMS

'For a man who had been out of practice for so many years, it was a splendid laugh, a most illustrious laugh. The father of a long line of brilliant laughs!'
'Scrooge was better than his word. He did it all, and ... more.' (Narrator)

FAMILY & RELATIONSHIPS

BRINGS RESPONSIBILITY

"... my clerk, with fifteen shillings a week, and a wife and family talking about a merry Christmas." (Scrooge)

BUT LONELINESS...

IS WORSE

"A solitary child, neglected by his friends, is left there still." (Ghost of Christmas Past)

"His partner lies upon the point of death, I hear; and there he sat alone. Quite alone in the world I do believe." (Belle's husband)

BRINGS PURPOSE

'When he thought that such another creature might have called him father ... his sight grew very dim indeed.' (Narrator)

CAN BE ADOPTIVE

'And to Tiny Tim, who did not die, he was a second father.' (Narrator)

FAMILY...

CAN HURT YOU

"Father is so much kinder to me than he used to be..." (Fan)

BRINGS LOSS

"'My little, little child!' cried Bob. He broke down all at once. He couldn't help it.' (Narrator)

CONTEXT

- With no birth control, families were large & financially burdensome.

- Often children from poor families had to work to make ends meet.

- The workhouse system often separated the most 'in need' families from loved ones.

DICKENS' VIEWPOINT

Dickens experienced family challenges. His father was in a debtor's jail & he was separated from his family.

Dickens had a large family as an adult (10 children!) & had to work hard to provide for them.

BECAUSE FAMILY...

IS LOVING

'... the two young Cratchits go upon his knees and laid, each child a little cheek, against his face.' (Narrator)

BRINGS JOY

'Wonderful games, wonderful unanimity, won-der-ful happiness!' (Narrator)

IS FORGIVING

"I couldn't be angry with him if I tried. Who suffers by his ill whims, Himself, always." (Fred)

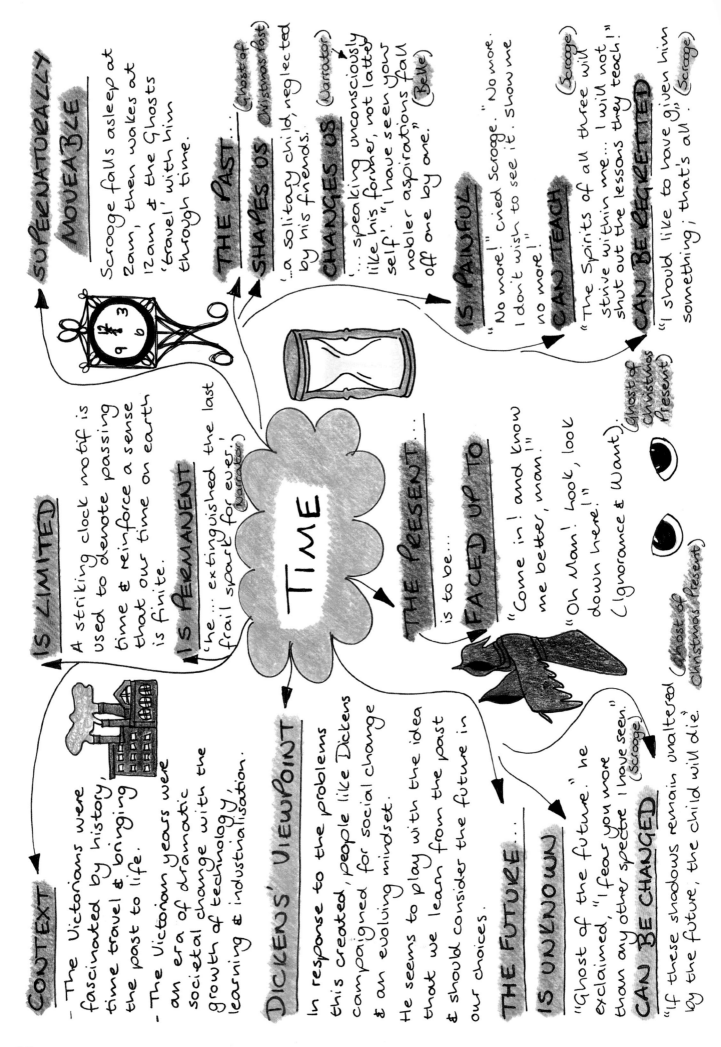

TIME

SUPERNATURALLY MOVEABLE

Scrooge falls asleep at 2am, then wakes at 12am & the Ghosts 'travel' with him through time.

THE PAST...

(Ghost of Christmas Past)

SHAPES US

"...a solitary child, neglected by his friends."
(Narrator)

CHANGES US

"...speaking unconsciously like his former, not latter self". "I have seen your nobler aspirations fall off one by one." *(Belle)*

IS PAINFUL

"No more!" cried Scrooge. "No more. I don't wish to see it. Show me no more!"
(Scrooge)

CAN TEACH

"The Spirits of all three strive within me... I will not shut out the lessons they teach!"
(Scrooge)

CAN BE REGRETTED

"I should like to have given him something; that's all." *(Scrooge)*

IS LIMITED

A striking clock motif is used to denote passing time & bringing a sense that our time on earth is finite.

IS PERMANENT

"he... extinguished the last frail spark for ever."
(Narrator)

CONTEXT

- The Victorians were fascinated by history, time travel & bringing the past to life.
- The Victorian years were an era of dramatic societal change with the growth of technology, learning & industrialisation.

DICKENS' VIEWPOINT

In response to the problems this created, people like Dickens campaigned for social change & an evolving mindset. He seems to play with the idea that we learn from the past & should consider the future in our choices.

THE FUTURE...

IS UNKNOWN

"Ghost of the future." he exclaimed. "I fear you more than any other spectre I have seen." *(Scrooge)*

CAN BE CHANGED

"If these shadows remain unaltered by the future, the child will die." *(Ghost of Christmas Present)*

THE PRESENT...

is to be...

FACED UP TO

"Come in! and know me better, man!"

"Oh Man! look, look down here!"
(Ignorance & Want).

(Ghost of Christmas Present)

FORM & STRUCTURE

HaHaHa!

DRAMATIC DEVICES

NARRATIVE VOICE

The narrator has a notably strong voice, or personality of its own.

He is **PERSONABLE** & speaks like a friend.

'If you should happen ... to know a man more blest in a laugh than Scrooge's nephew ... I should like to know him.'

He uses **COLLOQUIAL LANGUAGE** & is **DIRECT**

'Old Marley was dead as a door nail.'

'... and HUMOUR 'I might have been inclined, myself, to regard a coffin-nail as the deadest piece of ironmongery in the trade.'

He is all knowing, or **OMNISCIENT** carrying their dinners to the bakers' shops.'

His **HIGHLY DESCRIPTIVE** & **VIVID LANGUAGE** draws us into the story & uses the **FIVE SENSES** eg. 'thousand odours' & **LONG SENTENCES** to provide complexity.

STRONG CHARACTERISATION

makes the many that populate the story memorable. eg. 'fat, jovial voice' of Fezziwig & Dickens creates

SETTINGS full of colour and depth eg. 'A place where miners live, who labour in the bowels of the earth.'

A CHRISTMAS CAROL

- Is a 'ghost story' and a novella intended to be read aloud like a carol.

SIMPLE STRUCTURE

- Five Staves (or chapters) 'hung' on four ghost visitations. They are ...

- MARLEY.
- GHOST OF CHRISTMAS PAST.
- GHOST OF CHRISTMAS PRESENT.
- GHOST OF CHRISTMAS YET TO COME.

NON-LINEAR

- Moves between past, present & future.

CIRCULAR STRUCTURE

- Many of the ideas from Stave One are echoed/revisited in Stave Five (Fred's celebration, treatment of Bob Cratchit, attitude to Christmas, Charity collectors).

SOME HELPFUL SENTENCE STARTERS

- Dickens depicts/presents/ suggests/implies/employs/ represents/creates a sense of....

- The character of '...' is shown as/presented as....

- The word '...' shows us/ creates a sense of/creates a picture of....

- This alludes to/is reminiscent of/has echoes of/reminds us of/connotes...

- Similarly/likewise/ furthermore....

- Conversely....

- In contrast....

GAIN MAXIMUM MARKS

- Choose a quotation relevant to the question & point.

IN THE EXAM

- Consider how the quotation reflects character/theme/context.

- Explore in detail the impact of specific words or phrases.

- Evaluate how effective the author's choice of language is.

ANSWER THE QUESTION

- Read & understand what is being asked.

- Plan your answer.

- Refer to 5-6 quotes.

- Zoom in/focus in on key language/words.

- Discuss context if you have been told to.

DON'T FORGET....

- Use the best vocabulary you can.

- Use single quotation marks, unless the quote uses "speech."

- Check spelling & grammar.

EXAMPLES OF SPECIFIC LANGUAGE/LITERARY DEVICES IN THE NOVELLA

ADJECTIVE - a word describing a noun. eg '...a squeezing, wrenching, grasping, scraping, clutching, covetous old sinner.

ALLITERATION - the reoccurrence of the same letter or sound in adjacent or close words. eg '...secret, and self-contained, and solitary as an oyster.'

CHARACTONYM - where a character's given name gives a sense of their character. eg 'Cratchit' is evocative of an ordinary person scratching a living.

CLIFFHANGER - an ending to an episode or chapter that leaves you in suspense. eg at the end of Stave Three '(he)... beheld a solemn Phantom, draped and hooded, coming, like mist along the ground, towards him.'

CONTRAST - a comparison of difference. eg Scrooge's cold sternness in Stave One contrasts with his childish joy at the end of Stave Five.

DIALOGUE - the way the characters speak, revealing who they are eg 'Bah!' 'Humbug' in reference to Christmas.

DRAMATIC IRONY - when the reader knows something a character doesn't. eg that the grave is Scrooge's.

EMOTIVE LANGUAGE - words and phrases meant to evoke a strong emotional response. eg 'Where angels might have sat enthroned, devils lurked, and glared out menacing.'

EXCLAMATORY SENTENCES - the use of exclamation marks to convey strong emotion, sometimes mid-sentence. eg Ghost of Christmas Present, 'Come in! and know me better, man!'

FOIL - a character who contrasts with another character, usually the protagonist to highlight qualities of the other character. eg Fred to Scrooge.

FORESHADOWING - a warning or indication (of a future event). eg 'Marley was dead: to begin with,' foreshadows his ghostly appearance to Scrooge. '...he loved the child, and wished to keep him by his side, and dreaded he might be taken from him,' foreshadows Tiny Tim's death.

HYPERBOLE - exaggerated statements or claims not meant to be tak[en] literally. eg 'every idiot... should be boiled with his own pudding, and buried with a stake of holly through his heart.'

JUXTAPOSITION - two things being placed close together with contrastin[g] effect. eg The Christmas spirit of the nephew and Scrooge's 'Bah!' 'Humbug'. The abundance of the Gh[ost] of Christmas Present and the starving children beneath his robe. Scrooge's future death and Tiny Tim's

METAPHOR - One thing is described as another to paint a vivid picture.
eg 'A poor excuse for picking a man's pocket every twenty-fifth of December.'

MOOD - the tone and atmosphere created. eg the way Dickens varies mood through different points in Scrooge's journey with the Spirits.

MOTIF - an image or action repeated throughout the text. eg chiming bells to warn of visitors.

PATHETIC FALLACY - attribution of human feelings and responses to inanimate things or animals, especially in art and literature (weather). eg '... the weather sat in mournful meditation.'

PERSONIFICATION - where an object has human characteristics. eg 'Spanish onions... winking from their shelves in wanton slyness at the girls as they went by.'

REPETITION - The repeating of words or phrases for emphasis. eg 'Scroog[e] was his sole executor, his sole administrator, his sole assign, his sole residuary legatee, his sole friend, his sole mourner.'

RULE OF THREE - a method of using a trio of words to create a greater/more satisfying effect. eg 'unwatched, unwept, uncared for.'

SIMILE - a comparison using 'as' or 'like'. eg 'Solitary as an oyster.'

SENSORY DESCRIPTION - language that uses the five senses to paint a picture. eg 'moist and pulpy', 'blended scents of tea and coffee.'

SYMBOLISM - an image with a deeper, often recognisable meaning. eg Marley's chains symbolising his emotional 'shackling' to wealth and greed. The Ghost of Christmas Past's flame, symbolising 'illumination' of the past'.

SYNONYMS - the narrator uses long lists of words with similar meanings to emphasise a trait. eg '... a squeezing, wrenching, grasping, scraping, clutching...'